The Bake Sale Battle

Konrad Sharon Theo Tamara

Book Club

Paulette Trong Alicia Kyle

Pet Club

Ann Weil

Illustrated by Richard Hoit

Level Q Guided Reading Chapter Book

On Our Way to English: *The Bake Sale Battle*

© 2004 by Rigby
1000 Hart Road
Barrington, IL 60010
www.rigby.com

Text by Ann Weil
Illustrated by Richard Hoit

09 08 07 06 05 04 03
10 9 8 7 6 5 4 3 2 1

Printed in China

ISBN 0-7578-4403-0

Cast of Characters

Narrator

Alicia: President of the Pet Club

Kyle: Vice president of the Pet Club

Paulette: Pet Club member

Trong: Pet Club member

Tamara: Co-president of the Book Club

Theo: Co-president of the Book Club

Sharon: Book Club member

Konrad: Book Club member

Mr. Delgado: School teacher

Ms. Lok: School teacher

Students

Contents

Setting

Sunny Grove School

Scene I

Narrator: One afternoon at Sunny Grove School, the members of the Pet Club gathered together in Ms. Lok's room to discuss their plans for the year. Alicia was the president of the Pet Club, and her best friend, Kyle, was the vice president. Along with the other members, they made all of the decisions for the Pet Club.

Alicia: We've got a lot to go over today because we have to figure out how to raise money for the local animal shelter.

Kyle: The animal shelter needs money from the community in order to stay open and keep caring for the animals, but people haven't been giving much money recently.

Paulette: But that's terrible! If the animal shelter doesn't get enough money, the pets won't have a place to live anymore, and all those adorable animals will be homeless.

Alicia: That's why we need to figure out how to earn enough money to save the shelter. Now, who can share a great idea that will help us?

Trong: We could invent a new flavor of dog food and have a dog food sale.

Alicia: Could it be pizza-flavored?

Kyle: Um, I don't think that would work because not everyone has a dog, and many people don't even have pets. We probably wouldn't make enough money to help the shelter just by selling dog food—even pizza-flavored dog food.

Alicia: That's too bad because my dog always gets excited when the pizza delivery person comes to my house.

Paulette: OK, why don't we have a pet wash? People could bring their dirty pets to us, and we could give the pets baths.

Kyle: Um, no, I don't think that would work either because a pet wash would get too messy. Besides, cats clean themselves, so we would mostly be washing dogs. We probably wouldn't make much money doing that either, especially after we bought the special animal shampoo . . .

Alicia: But Kyle, we've got to do *something,* or we won't make any money for the animal shelter. Hey, do you remember those great cookies you brought to lunch and shared with us the other day?

Kyle: Do you mean the ones I made from my grandmother's recipe? Yeah, I remember that I didn't have enough patience to wait for the cookies to finish baking, and . . .

Alicia: And they were all soft and delicious in the middle! They were the absolute best chocolate-chip cookies I've ever tasted, so why don't we have a bake sale and sell those delicious treats?

Scene II

Narrator: In Mr. Delgado's classroom, the members of the school's Book Club were having a meeting to talk about the need to purchase more books for the Children's Library. Theo and Tamara were in charge of this group, and their friends Sharon and Konrad were new members.

Tamara: We still need a plan to earn some money, or we won't be able to buy any books for the Children's Library.

Theo: Last night I was reading a book about small businesses, and the book had some very good suggestions for making money. I brought the book with me, in case we need it.

Konrad: Theo, that book looks like it weighs more than all of my schoolbooks and yours put together. We'll never have enough time to read it.

Tamara: I enjoy reading, too, Theo, but in order to save time, we should probably come up with our own ideas.

Sharon: Hey, what if we have a bake sale? We could make double-chocolate brownies and sell them during lunchtime.

Tamara: That's a splendid idea, and I can even bake the brownies at my grandfather's bakery!

Theo: You know, Tamara, my family has tons of cookbooks at home. I could bring in a few of them tomorrow. Then we could all read them together, select the best brownie recipe, taste test them, and . . .

Tamara: Once again, Theo, I don't think there's enough time for all of that. Anyway, my grandfather has the best recipes.

Theo: Actually, just last week, I was reading a book about grandparents, and it said that . . .

Narrator: That settled it: The Book Club decided they would have the best bake sale ever and raise more than enough money to buy hundreds and hundreds of books for the Children's Library!

Scene I

Narrator: Both the Book Club and the Pet Club planned their bake sales for lunchtime on the same Wednesday. Neither club realized that the other had come up with the same idea for the same day. Alicia, Kyle, Trong, and Paulette arrived first to begin setting up the Pet Club table in the cafeteria before everyone arrived for lunch.

Trong: Kyle, these cookies are fantastic.

Alicia: These are truly the best chocolate-chip cookies in the world. We'd better start selling them soon or we'll eat them all up ourselves.

Kyle: I don't think they taste exactly the same as my grandmother's. I think I was supposed to add the sugar *before* I put in the eggs, and . . .

Alicia: I think our bake sale is going to be a complete and total success, so let's hurry and finish getting everything ready.

Narrator: The members of the Book Club arrived soon to set up their table in the cafeteria. They were in such a hurry as they carried in boxes of brownies that they didn't notice the Pet Club table.

Tamara: Now we're late, Theo, and it's all your fault.

Theo: I'm sorry, but I had to go back upstairs because I left my book *How to Sell Anything to Anybody* in my locker, and . . .

Tamara: And I told you that we don't need a how-to book on selling things to run a bake sale. We're selling brownies, not cars.

Sharon: Actually, Theo's book may help us because on page 4 it says that it's very important to picture success.

Konrad: Theo, what does that mean, "picture success"?

Theo: It means that we should have a picture in our mind of us selling lots of brownies and making piles of money to buy boxes of books to give to the Children's Library.

Narrator: As Tamara tried to picture success, she slowly gazed around the lunchroom and noticed the Pet Club table.

Tamara: Right now I'm picturing that we have a very large problem.

Theo: Well, that's not what the book says you're supposed to do, Tamara. It says right here on page 5 that it's necessary to think positively if you want to be successful.

Narrator: Tamara tapped Theo on the shoulder so he would look up from his book and then pointed over to where Kyle, Alicia, Trong, and Paulette were putting the finishing touches on their bake sale table. When the Book Club saw the Pet Club poster on the front of the table, Sharon sighed in frustration and Konrad frowned with worry.

Theo: Uh-oh, now I see what you mean.

Sharon: What are we going to do?

Theo: I think we'd better try to find something in my book about this sort of situation.

Narrator: Theo quickly flipped through the pages of his book, looking for a solution to their problem, as students began arriving in the lunchroom.

Konrad: We need to hurry and get set up quickly. Everyone's coming to lunch now, and if we're not ready, they'll go straight to the Pet Club table to buy their cookies.

Theo: Here, I found the answer we're looking for! I checked the index and there's an entire chapter on how to beat other businesses. Let's see, first we need to find out who would want our brownies. They are our target audience.

Tamara: No, first we need to find our sign! Theo, please stop reading and help us get everything ready.

Narrator: Tamara found the sign lying on the floor under the table and Sharon and Konrad taped it to the front of the table. Theo kept peeking at his book when he thought no one was watching him.

Scene II

Narrator: Meanwhile the Pet Club members had also noticed the Book Club's bake sale table. Alicia tried to cheer Kyle up because he had a gloomy look on his face.

Kyle: Their brownies are probably better than my cookies, so maybe we should just quit now.

Alicia: What are you talking about, Kyle? Your cookies are the best, and besides, we can't give up before we even get started.

Paulette: Yeah, Kyle, as soon as people bite into one of your cookies, they'll come running back for more.

Narrator: A few students began buying cookies from the Pet Club, and soon the money was piling up. The members of the Book Club were still waiting for their first customer, and Tamara grew impatient as Theo continued to flip through the pages of his book.

Tamara: Look, they're buying cookies from the Pet Club instead of buying our brownies! What are we going to do?

Theo: Hey, this chapter called "How to Price Your Product" just gave me an idea!

Narrator: Theo grabbed a marker and changed the price of the Book Club's brownies from 25 cents to 20 cents.

Theo: Brownies, get your delicious, homemade double-chocolate brownies for only *twenty* cents!

Narrator: Suddenly, all of the students who were in line to buy cookies from the Pet Club rushed over to the Book Club table to buy brownies.

Alicia: If we don't reduce our price the same way the Book Club did, no one will buy our delicious cookies!

Narrator: Trong and Paulette lowered the price of Pet Club cookies to 19 cents, and the students rushed back to the Pet Club table. Each club continued to reduce the price of the cookies and the brownies, and the students ran from one table to the other, getting dizzy in the bake sale battle.

Tamara: Our delicious brownies are only *fifteen* cents!

Kyle: Our cookies are only *ten* cents!

Theo: Our brownies are just a *nickel!*

Narrator: Soon both clubs were giving their cookies and brownies away for free. They were trying so hard to beat each other that they'd totally forgotten their goals of making money to support their charities. When the bell rang, signaling the end of lunchtime, both tables were out of cookies and brownies, but neither club had made much money.

Alicia: I can't wait to see how much money we made!

Trong: Let's see . . . 4 dollars . . . and 15 cents.

Alicia: Is that all? But we thought we'd make much more money than that! We won't be able to save the animal shelter with only $4.15. What happened?

Kyle: What happened is that we were giving our cookies away rather than selling them! If the Book Club hadn't made us lower our prices so much, we would have made much more money.

Narrator: The Book Club members were just as unhappy with the results of their bake sale. Theo counted the money, and Tamara swept brownie crumbs into an empty box as Sharon and Konrad took down the sign.

Konrad: I thought the bake sale would be so much fun and we would make tons of money to buy books for the Children's Library. I was already imagining the children's excitement as they saw all the new books.

How to Sell Anything to Anybody

Sharon: We don't even have enough money here to buy a comic book.

Tamara: I had everything planned out perfectly, so I just don't know what could have gone wrong.

Theo: According to my budget, if you subtract the money we paid for the ingredients used to make the brownies, we actually *lost* money.

Narrator: As both clubs finished cleaning up, Mr. Delgado and Ms. Lok watched the clubs move the tables back to where they belonged. Sharon, Konrad, Trong, and Paulette left for their next class, while Kyle, Alicia, Tamara, and Theo finished packing everything up. They all looked as if this had been the worst day of their lives.

Mr. Delgado: So, how did your bake sales go today?

Alicia: Ours didn't go very well, since we only earned about four dollars.

Theo: So did we, and if you subtract the cost of our supplies . . .

Tamara: . . . we made absolutely nothing.

Kyle: It was your fault for lowering your brownie prices so much!

Tamara: But your cookie prices were lowered, too!

Ms. Lok: I think you're all forgetting something. You're supposed to be trying to help the community through your bake sales. I think you should all use some creativity and intelligence to figure out a better way for each group to reach its goals.

Act III

Scene I

Narrator: That afternoon after school, Kyle and Alicia sat outside in the shade of a tree, discussing the bake sale.

Kyle: It was probably a bad idea to keep cutting the price of the cookies, but at the time it didn't seem like we could do anything else.

Alicia: Your cookies were so good that we could have kept selling them for 25 cents each. But I was so busy thinking about how to beat the Book Club that I completely forgot about helping the animal shelter.

Narrator: Soon Theo and Tamara walked by and stopped to talk to Kyle and Alicia.

Theo: I'm sorry about what happened with the bake sales today. I thought selling our brownies for less was a good idea at the time, but then we got carried away.

Kyle: It wasn't all your fault—we lowered our prices, too. We ended up with no money for the animal shelter.

Tamara: We don't have any money for the Children's Library either.

Kyle: I guess we'll have to think of a new idea to raise money for the animal shelter.

Tamara: And we'll have to come up with another way to make money to buy new books for the Children's Library.

Alicia: I think I have an idea about how we can make enough money for *both*.

Narrator: Alicia was about to tell everyone her idea when she stopped Mr. Delgado and Ms. Lok as they were on their way to the parking lot.

Alicia: I think I figured out a way for both clubs to make money, but we'll need permission to have another bake sale.

Everyone: You want to have another bake sale, Alicia?

Alicia: Yes, but this time we'll combine our clubs and have one giant, wonderful bake sale. Then we'll split all the money we make between the Children's Library and the animal shelter.

Narrator: They all cheered when they heard Alicia's great idea (even Mr. Delgado and Ms. Lok), and the teachers agreed to get permission for the two clubs to have another bake sale at lunchtime.

Scene II

Narrator: A week later, the members of both clubs hosted another bake sale, but this time they all worked together.

Tamara: I think we're selling even more sweets than last time, and we're charging full price for everything. We'll make enough money to buy lots of books for the Children's Library.

Alicia: We'll also make enough money to help the animal shelter give food and homes to plenty of poor animals.

Tamara: I asked my parents, and they said I could adopt a kitten from the animal shelter for my birthday.

Theo: I have lots of pet-care books at home that you can borrow if you want.

Tamara: But you don't even own a pet.

Theo: I decided to do some research before making a decision. I like animals almost as much as I like books.

Best
Chocolate Chip
Cookies and
Double Fudge
Brownies
ever!
25¢
Every penny helps
animals and buys
books for children!

okies and Brownies

Narrator: By the end of lunchtime, all the cookies and brownies had been sold. The two clubs divided the money evenly, donating one half to the animal shelter and the other half to the Children's Library.

Konrad: This bake sale was a complete success, thanks to Kyle's cookies, Tamara's brownies, and Alicia's idea to work together.

Theo: I think our bake sale made even more money than my business book predicted that we would!

Narrator: As the last students left the cafeteria, Mr. Delgado and Ms. Lok stopped by the table to help the two clubs clean up.

Mr. Delgado: We're very proud of all of you for working so well together.

Kyle: It would have been so much easier—and more profitable—if we had figured it out at the beginning.

Tamara: And it also would have been a lot more fun!

Alicia: Speaking of fun, Kyle and I were talking about starting a soccer club, and we wanted to know if you all would like to be in it with us.

Kyle: You probably wouldn't be interested, but . . .

Theo: I have the greatest book that we can all use to help us play soccer better!

Tamara: We'll need to raise money for the equipment. . . . How about having another bake sale?